GLOBALLY CONSCIOUS SPIRIT, LOCALLY MINDFUL CITIZEN

Dalena Lorenzo

Amazon - May 25, 2024

CONTENTS

Title Page
PREFACE — 1
SPIRITUAL GEOGRAPHIES & YOUR PERSONAL IDENTITY — 5
REALISING THE PAST; RELEASING MEMORIES TO KNOW FOR THE FUTURE — 11
CONSCIOUSLY PARTICIPATING IN OR TRANSFORMING ESTABLISHED INSTITUTIONS TO ALLOW SPIRIT TO EMERGE — 15
CONSCIOUSLY SPIRITUAL PHILANTHROPY, LOVINGLY MINDFUL SOCIETY BUILDING — 20
CONSCIOUS SELF-RULE & MINDFUL POLICING — 23
CONSCIOUS SPIRITUAL HEALTH & MINDFUL MEDITATION — 25
POSTFACE — 29

PREFACE

This treatise is an exploration of what it means to be a globally conscious spirit & locally mindful citizen. In many manners it is about finding yourself where you are on this earth & what it is possible for you to do to contribute to your society, starting at home while being aware of the worldly connectedness of yourself with others on this planet where we live together in some relationship with nature.

Each generation inherits institutional structures from their forebears that allow them to vote, enjoy health benefits, & otherwise enjoy their voice in legal systems with a view to modifications of them if necessary. Often we find ourselves having mindful thoughts that may or may not be original but have often been thought before by great philosophers. Since we are part of the inheritors of the wisdom of these great societies preceding us, we often consciously intuit their wisdom as its seeps through to us through the ether, as it were, & appropriate it as our own.

But it is necessary to recognize the origins of our thoughts in the passed down teachings of our esteemed Liberal Arts education system, as well as give credit where credit is due to ourselves &

our own potentially original thoughts by writing them down in our essays for professors who then subject them to peer review so they are not a random anarchy of disparate meaningless voices in the chaotic unstructured stratosphere of social media. We must force ourselves to dig deeper into our own sentiments & engage in dialogue with our peers to develop our ideas so as to contribute to society rather than merely throwing undeveloped opinions into the fray where they will be lost or misinterpreted in a milieu of so called fake news. You cannot effectively contribute to society unless you are by rare chance a prolific busker in the various forms of social media available for participation.

On the contrary, this author is subjectively writing from a western perspective with roots in ancient Greece, where

Ideally, the polis was a corporation of citizens who all participated in its government, religious cults, defense, and economic welfare and who obeyed its sacred and customary laws. The citizens actually governed in varying degrees, depending upon the form of government—e.g., tyranny, oligarchy, aristocracy, or democracy (https://www.britannica.com/topic/polis).

Greece itself is a consciously mindful rules-based Balkan country that was at the intersection of a variety of different politicized cultures that came to reflect in society as so called cults, or what we now know as spiritual/religious wisdom learnings. Greece also was in sufferance of being the victim of conflicts between those cultures, often fanatical, a condition that persists in the mediterranean region to this day. Yet it manage to mediate those conflicts & develop from different cultural traditions the muscle of liberal democracy as it would eventually evolve. Even cultures as disparate as African, Egyptian, Mesopotamian, Zoroastrian, Buddhist, Hindu & Taoist contributed to the Greek form of democracy (https://www.europeanproceedings.com/article/10.15405/

epsbs.2021.05.37). This allowed also a tolerance of different voices & narratives to exist together in consciously mindful harmony & emanate outward to the rest of the world, particularly the democratic Europe & North America today. Today Greece, alongside Italy with its own heritage, remain the most stable of Balkan countries.

The important lesson from this treatise is that one consciously & mindfully finds where one fits in their society, through recognizing the familiarity of their roots, & then proceeds to enliven & rejuvenate their local community. They can do this in not only a spirit of tolerance for other narrative cultures & identities but also a tolerance of the legacies of different democratic institutions, building on their weaknesses & emboldening their strengths, starting with themselves as a unified field of spiritual consciousness that is globally mindful.

In this sense, the first chapter will deal with contextual geographies to help situate the individual citizen culturally & spiritually. The second chapter will face the issue of time experienced by the collective race & individual persons. The third chapter will deal with consciously facing our culturally based institutional challenges in democracies & authoritarian regimes, allowing citizens to develop or transform them from subjective effort (eg. mindful voting) & objective consensus (conscious democracy) more or less within the system as it is. The fourth chapter explores the potential for mindful philanthropy & how it can reflect our spiritual evolution. The fifth chapter will deal with our rules based system, the chance for mindful self policing (consciously cooperative with police), the ego limits & consciousness potentialities of our legal system. The sixth & final chapter will deal with holistic solutions for conscious spiritual health & mindful meditation, to allow the individual citizen to dig deeper into their emotions & intellect so

DALENA LORENZO

as to consciously reflect positively in their mindfully chosen society.

SPIRITUAL GEOGRAPHIES & YOUR PERSONAL IDENTITY

In today's world it is often not easy to realize where one belongs. We have many structural contexts surrounding the individual, the family, the community & the nation, even regions & continents. Identity is increasingly fragmented by proliferating narratives of perceived personal willpower, leading to changes in gender, name & even plastic surgery. While this is not a diatribe against personal identity choice, it can complicate people's journey through life, confuse & displace others by virtue of unfair physical advantage - in trans sports, for example.

In many cases, these periphery identity dilemmas are in situations of suppressed willpower & repressed sexuality that reaches a boiling point & needs to be channeled, released & recognized in some structural manner. Hopefully, educators can recognize these personal issues at some stage of the learning process & address them without discrimination or emotional dissonance, otherwise they may strain the system in excessive proliferation of multiple personalities. This occurs leading to meaninglessness &

nihilism in our physical & emotional places in our own structures that have existed for centuries & worked for the most part, for us.

This could be more true of the rules based system in the Liberal west where tolerance for others' identity choices is more entrenched in the system of human rights. But even these relatively advanced systems are being vigourously challenged by Nietszchean style assertions of personal will to power that may threaten to increase, to say the least, dissonance in our inclusive society, & violently deconstruct institutions that are otherwise tolerant & adaptable. The end result could be a new kind of sexual authoritarianism that is a throwback to the middle ages world of harsh discipline & punishment. It is in many senses a backlash against misogyny but could also be a reassertion of misogyny, as the opposite sexes decide to depart relationships, even friendly ones, in a polarized struggle for power, as we are witnessing happen in Christian Russia today.

In this sense, the appeal of Islam with sharply defined roles for men & women, may attract some segments of society as a counter to proliferating multiple sexualities. On the other hand, the rigidness of Islam my exacerbate bipolarities in the relationship between the two basic sexes. On the other hand, liberal Islam is also evolving but is in sufferance of steps back, the result of conflict or authoritarianism destroying it, for example, in Bosnia & Turkije, respectively. Political instability is exploited by the military in liberal Egypt & Pakistan, two leading Islamic democracies.

It is not probable that LGBT communities can survive in the short time frame even in Liberal Islam, let alone fanatical Islam, heightening the appeal of this religion for those who doubt such lifestyle choices. In the meantime, Liberal Europe & North America, as well as some south Asian countries, are struggling to include or repress new sexual identities, sometimes with no thought for how this could upend structure or later channel negatively within the system. Educators could do well to introduce inclusive sexual wellness & mindfulness training for the mature that is palatable in some manner, rather through art & erotica than porn. Porn tends to exacerbate sexual stereotypes in its current form instead of encouraging loving relationships & fun physical fitness. It could go without saying that often once these venues are opened to mature individuals they can find there is available a conduit for their own particular emotions in a manner that respects others & minimizes harm or master-slave role-playing.

Now all this is about, in a sense, regulating our lower natures that swell up into the personality demanding expression & respect. It is also about fitness & mental wellness, since we are of multiple natures ourselves; sexual, intellectual & spiritual. In the far east Indian sub continent, these are known as *chakras*, & one is encouraged to explore these physical realities in more depth than can be explained here. One could find that there are eastern wisdom traditions in for example, Zoroastrianism, Hinduism & Buddhism, that offer a manifold explanation of human nature that accounts for complexities we may recognize in our particular character predilections that are seemingly not respected by society at large, let alone in modern day India even.

Such venues are openly accessible in the Liberal west, but our blessedly secular society so tolerant of spiritualities tends to not encourage them enough as a form of formal identification. Currently we are struggling with identifying our lower natures as a measure of identity, while the higher natures remain unobjectifiable, & perhaps should so remain. Perhaps, in a similar manner, some people would also prefer not to objectify themselves the result of changing personalities in time & cumbersome bureaucratic paperwork this entails. Conversely many people may consider that they would fit into some generalisable identity that is of course, flexible, while simultaneously allowing mindful fun harmony between sexuality & spirituality. This would allow the expression of consciousness to expand in woken up personalities/ individualities, as it were.

Liberal Societies

In a further sense, the failure of secular Liberal society to satisfy religious identity expression, the result of exclusive religious fanatics, has left segments of the population without accessible means of spiritual expression, that is suppressed into identifiable sexual outlets. Means to allow people to discover their respective faiths could have a positive effect on sexual expression, but this remains a taboo subject in many religions where sexuality is a suppressed lower nature. Yet the aesthetics of many religions bely the beauty of sexuality itself & should be more openly discussed with rational composure.

A good manner to situate unexpressed sexual, religious or spiritual sentiments would be the United Nation's (UN) definition of intangible cultural heritage, that are admittedly difficult to define cultural phenomena. Escaping objectification was once a women's prerogative, while now there is a rush to define one's personal identity at different temporal places ad nauseum, rather than merely subscribing to private protected individualities. The need to constantly express ones' private sexuality ends up as nothing other than a decadent frivolity in its ultimate translation in culture as the end result. What does it mean if an identity is there today & gone tomorrow --- is it merely as fleeting as human existence itself, or is it a measure of a more enduring personality, perhaps even a longer life --- Further, there are otherwise plenty of means of expression that are palatable & impressive to others in society without encroaching on one another's personal space.

Individual people of today's social media culture could prefer & enjoy Canada's anarchic 'tossed salad' multiculturalism, where individualities sometimes thrive in notional enclaves apart from one another, a postmodern phenomena that could lend itself to regional fragmentation. The failure of successive 'liberal' governments to maintain an inclusive national narrative is part of the problem. In the USA postmodernism has contributed to the bi-polarising of politicised cultural narratives, where a 'melting pot' multiculturalism was the result of a holistic narrative of national unity that normally tends to prevail based on a longer common history. The desire to generate history, particularly in Canada, could indeed forge national unity, but it instead defers to the prevalence of people's individual personal or group histories.

This stems ironically, in part, from Canada's proximity to the relatively anarchic cultures of Europe, where unity is a measure also of structuralised anarchy in the European Union. This is also reflected in states' anarchy within the USA, but the national narrative, sometimes unsuccessfully, diminishes state individuality. Yet Europe remains more unified culturally in many manners than its different North American reflections, & Mexico is most similar to a culturally & racially homogenous individual European state among similar states.

On the other hand, Canada & the USA incorporate races & cultures from around the globe that are notably different from one another & yet are not totally easy to manage in the context of multiple mutual reconcilements. These disparate cultures, as well as indigenous populations that were initially displaced by European settlements, must settle on a unity of national narrative that adequately respects their rights without allowing foreign authoritarian regimes to exploit their related diasporas. Similarly, North American & European sovereignties should carefully measure the extent that their global influence precludes other entities of their national expression, patriotism & development. So far, the Liberal rules based system, while stemming from Europe, also modified Europe in its own image, to one of more accountable inclusivity, & it remains the best democratic system we have.

In choosing one's identity, it is necessary to measure one's immediate context, while admittedly potentially limited, & consider that one was born by choice or karma in a particular location, in a particular family, a particular faith, to engage in contextual spiritual cultural lessons that they offer. This proscribes a more manageable context that can minimize the stress of the vagaries of our personalities & channel them in an effective manner within even patriotic society as it exists about one.

REALISING THE PAST; RELEASING MEMORIES TO KNOW FOR THE FUTURE

The human race has arrived at a cross point in its collective heritage, whether it can make a learned transition successfully into a new age, or be bogged down in the failures of the past. It is not the first time such a point has been reached, & at various stages in history, humanity has been faced with choices about movement forth it had to make. Centuries of education were presented to us, it is only what we have digested from them that could allow us to progress into the future. It is thus our memories that permit us to live in the now & tomorrow, a respect for our past as it were. In this sense, our notion of time is not so linear but is simultaneously a confluence of the past, the present & unfolding events. It must be emphasized that we can vividly live past successes in the present, now, & into the time ahead. This is not necessarily the secret to time travel but a common sense assertion that allows us to more easily grasp the nature of our place in time itself.

The title of this chapter - 'Realising the Past; Releasing Memories to Know for the Future' - is not an assertion set in stone, but are fluid & interchangeable verbiages. It could perhaps be a better title - 'Releasing the Past; Realising Memories for the Future' - but there is a subtle difference in emphasis. For, if the past were to be released, the weakness in our human nature would choose to relive those times when we were in power, rather than simply & humbly at one with & knowing ourselves. Therefore it is necessary to remember when we were realising ourselves in the past rather than set ourselves free in *will to power* & knowledge activities. Not that such activities are all bad, since powerful people have helped to push humanity into the future in wise manners.

Conversely, releasing the past could be interpreted as simply *letting go* of the past's failures & relegating them to historical lessons learned. Instead we choose here to attempt to realise the past in a twofold manner, that simultaneously witnesses past failures & builds on past successes, allowing/releasing our positive memories to live on & enhance the past now through knowing. This occurs at the macro & micro levels, in our collective unified experiences as the human race & in our personal individual experiences reflective of that what is greater than ourselves. We must clearly see the past, digest it rather than forget it & build from it to allow us to live to the best of our lives. We can, in the process, find ourselves in unusual times where we experience deja vu in a pleasant & positive manner, while, at other times, be astounded by newfound experiences enlivening in manners never before perceived but pure & innocent in essence, as birth vision is a will to an entry into worlds never before seen or known.

From Memory to Will to Gnosis

There is an interpretation of the Gnosis faith from the past (2nd century) that sees it as a 'halfway house between philosophic paganism and Christianity'; & sees a more pronounced division between humanity & G-d. There are all sorts of heresies & spirit diversions that seem pagan. It is more skeptical of the relationship between humans & G-d than most religions are, yet often espouses a Manichean (good vs. evil) perspective of the universe. Revelation is a more strenuous process than meditation & there are all sorts of traps & pitfalls along the way, compounded by humanity's antagonistic relationship with an antagonistic G-d aloof from an earth 'he' did not conceptualise.

That is an account of the received wisdom in reference to Gnosis. From this point we add the word meaning 'speculative' in relation to the word gnosis, understood as simply 'knowing' without the historical baggage. Speculative, it is asserted here, means knowing in the capacity to see & know clearly & willfully, as in the visualization capacity inherent in comprehending the spiritual nature. In fact, at the time of the late 14th century, the word speculative had this precise meaning in human gnosis or knowing/experiencing G-d itself as an act of individual empowerment in time.

Of historical significance in 1215, the Magna Carta had been signed, perhaps for the first time in world heritage held a Monarch to democratic account. Some knowledgeable enlightenment had happened, even then. For man had reckoned with the G-dhead itself & perhaps released his own spirituality from repression by non-faithful Monarchic mediations with G-d. Since then, the Crown's honour can be held to account in negotiations if not judged to be in good faith.

Yet the time was no doubt remaining in the dark middle ages, but by the transition from the 14th century 'Renaissance' to the 17th century 'Enlightenment', the word speculative's meaning changed dramatically, as did the meaning of the word enlightenment as a memory. No more was speculative about gnosis or knowing, but had come to mean 'theoretical' or 'conjectural' in intellectual assertion, & this meaning remains to this day.

In a positive sense, this meant humble & unassuming rather than the arrogance of assertively claiming total knowledge or gnosis, as Plotinus observed in the 3rd century C.E. Conversely, the word enlightenment was not about being illumined by G-d through grace & revelation but about total willful knowledge of a sort determined through the power of inductive logic in the space of time by man, to, of course develop preconceived deductive theories (memories) into the further future. Enlightenment tended to mean total science devoid of any spurious connection with the divine. Nor in its searches could it find any evidence of G-d itself in time, but only evidence of man in nature's history. In this sense, the seeds of the enlightenment may have been planted by those of the gnosis faith in their doubts about G-d & sometimes rationalist assertions about a cruel heritage of nature. The gnosis lesson for humanity here is that such memories can allow collective being into the future while being less skeptical about the truth of G-d & its relation with human spirit.

CONSCIOUSLY PARTICIPATING IN OR TRANSFORMING ESTABLISHED INSTITUTIONS TO ALLOW SPIRIT TO EMERGE

Clearly, we should utilise knowing being in faith together with rational memory to consciously face our culturally based institutional challenges in democracies & authoritarian regimes, to allow citizens to develop or transform them from subjective effort (eg. mindful voting) & objective consensus (conscious democracy led by the elected). From this it is possible that a new spirituality will emerge, where individuals co exist in harmony & spirit without the excessive constraints of the moral limitations of our existing rules-based system. Instead people should evolve to a state of consciousness where they automatically intuit & respect one another's rights in a transcendent sphere of mutually beneficent relationships. This win-win situation should be subject to constant negotiation, facilitation & mediation but on a more intuitive level than merely abiding by laws. In fact, it would go beyond law abiding citizens contributions by merely working & voting to spontaneous demonstrations of faith in one another & G-d as well as increasing personal & institutional acts of philanthropy or equitable distribution of resources across all strata of societies.

Enlightened International Bodies

In fact we can ironically find the roots of these institutional transformations of domestic state societies in customary international law & international organizations, including three state sovereignties that have given much inspiration to the rest for the world, the USA, Canada & Europe. The Declaration of Independence & the latter two Charters of Human Rights set the precedent for the establishment of the UN, as well as regional bodies from the EU, the Organization for Security & Cooperation in Europe (OSCE), the Organization of African States (OAS), the Association of South East Asian Nations (ASEAN) & Inter-American Human Rights (IAHR) System in Latin America.

All of these institutions reflect some measure of hard international law so much as states have ratified their conventions & funded their hierarchy (eg. The UN). Regional organizations exist relatively to one another, as states do without mutual treaties, in a state of customary international law, that is in soft law, that sometimes fall short of politically binding relations. It is unfortunate that states cannot spontaneously & philanthropically get along with one another & require treaties & more binding international conventions to regulate their behaviour. & this remains mostly undeveloped & customary in nature. One regional institution (OSCE) seeks to surpass various interests & seemingly stifling hierarchies by establishing a system of inter-state consensus building with a leadership that regularly rotates from state to state not depending on relatively hierarchical state power parities.

This is truly an example of enlightened horizontal leadership formulation, with procedures & operations of minimal hierarchy & fluidity of semi-hierarchical facilitative leadership relations within the rotating chairmanship than the more rigidly top down foundation of the UN headed by the exclusive Security Council vs. the more democratic General Assembly. This is a testament to European culture but also to global culture since many nations outside of Europe belong to more fluid, consensual & facilitative OSCE, including Canada, the USA & even Russia. While OSCE has not been able to surpass some recent European conflicts (Ukraine-Russia/Armenia-Azerbaijan), it has mechanisms designed to be utilized to surpass those conflicts even at its weak peripheries, it therefore remains a matter of the collective political will of its leading members to participate in OSCE & utilize its available tools, setting an example to other fragmented regions, from the Middle East & Africa, even South Asia & South America where narcotics eat away internally at their host states & emanate negatively outward to other regions across the globe.

Notably, many internal national state legislations reflect implementation of existing UN norms, but & it is unfortunate OSCE has not been able to mirror those in a more hierarchical Europe as effectively since it is so customary in its practice of law, so as not to offend anyone. In effect, OSCE is similar to a giant commune or a Kibbutz while asserting regional identity in a positive, consensual & inclusive manner. Perhaps it is not meant to be such hard law for it could instead softly reflect what we have spoken about here, of a more intuitive system of relationships between individuals, & by extension, of states. A minimal number of treaties between states can be simpler but many know that even marriages sometimes require rigourous prenuptials.

One example of multiple yet simplified treaties regulating periphery relations is the *49th parallel* between Canada & the USA, the longest undefended border in the world. Canada also serves as a diplomatic connection to Europe that does not suffer the same extent of historical dissonance with the continent that the US does. Thus Canada can be an effective peacekeeper between Europe & the US. The *Schengen regime* in Europe is similar multi-border reflection of the 49th parallel, allowing the free passage of goods & persons with minimal identity checks. But since such entities are mostly often bogged down in the seemingly slow-paced but necessary legally plodding relations of oversight (eg. US Congress), it is only voting that releases the inspiration of various styles of leadership (our choice here is of consensual/horizontal/facilitative democracies), sometimes including even more hierarchical monarchies, to motivate masses to the conscious discipline or even mindful leisure of their chosen sexualities or spiritualities. Perhaps for OSCE to succeed in the harmony of the European unity project more faith is needed in its institutional mechanisms, & G-d willing in G-d itself.

Clearly, there are not enough harmonies & doves in the world. In Canada - a relatively farsighted & enlightened pacific player in the democratic West - a proposed Department of Peace has not yet been formed. Canada now prioritizes peacekeeping through NATO rather than the UN Blue Helmets or regional OSCE (north west) & is perhaps too slowly harmonizing domestic laws with precisely principled international ones. For example, the UN's Universal Declaration of Human Rights (UDHR) starts *'with an acknowledgement that we have responsibilities toward each other. It includes rights that, say, the Canadian Charter does not, such as the "right to own property", the "right to form and join trade unions"… The vision is of a just society, not only a free one'* (Father Raymond J. De Souza, 'The Universal Declaration of Human Rights - a rare light in a dark century', <u>The National Post</u>, 10/12/2023). A recent survey asked *'respondents if they had [comprehended] the Canadian Charter of Rights & Freedoms… signed in 1982, and 33 percent answered they had'* (Stephanie Taylor, 'People are confused: Survey suggests Canadians need education on Charter rights', *Canadian Press*; 10/12/2023). Building history in Canada should not only start with people asserting their human rights within the framework of the Canadian Charter but also reflective of ratifications of the UN's Rights system.

CONSCIOUSLY SPIRITUAL PHILANTHROPY, LOVINGLY MINDFUL SOCIETY BUILDING

A fine example of global philanthropy outside of countries & beyond member states' domestic social programs is the United Nations' Sustainable Development Goals (SDG) Impact Fund that now has 10 Billion USD in assets. Yet this still reflects a small percentage of the Gross National Income (GNI) of its member states. Even the US that has until recently contributed annually nearly 64 Billion USD, this is a fraction of 1% of it's GNI. In theory, this includes monies to be released given structural adjustment by the recipients; a true effort at societal if not civilization-building itself. Presumably societies & governments will internalize this international charity into education & social programs that complement, embolden & encourage free competition with all its exercises in the growth of Gross Domestic Product (GDP).

What this chapter is more about is how to develop such a macro-strategy on the micro-personal & eventually spiritual level. While trillionaires & billionaires know that their contributions to charitable or philanthropic foundations, including those of their own generation, will impact society, as the UN does itself, these results can be a lesson for all of us. Most importantly, it is a lesson in the personal development of love & care for one another. We must develop higher spiritual expectations of ourselves & what we can give to society for mutual win-win outcomes. This is the notion of enlightened self-interest for when you give you witness your returns to society within yourself as well as your environment.
That is, you are a spiritually conscious reflection of the society you build & perhaps also pay taxes within a system that balances free competition with loving & nourishing spirit itself.

As our structure of personal being evolves, we incorporate our tolerance for others in society thus nourishing ourselves & growing together as one spiritual people. We are conscious of our historical mistakes as well as what works in our memories to enliven our progress forthwith. We develop a personal spiritual wealth that allows us to give to society where there are gaps in taxation or can contribute to changing the system to be more accountable & benevolent to taxpayers struggling to participate in the free marketplace. In this sense, tolerant care for others is tolerant care for yourself, particularly as the population ages the youth must eventually take care of their elders if they are not by that time self-sufficient. That is one important example of need. But it is more empowering to visualize society as a holistic spiritual macro-organism that benefits immensely & progresses from the loving participation of citizens in it. In that manner the structure of society's being evolves as individuals evolve to make a difference now for tomorrow through the development of love in one's heart & spirit. We must focus our work in the mindfulness of how it contributes to the whole system of our evolution of holy togetherness.

The question of accountability rises again in our minds as we look at ourselves to see how much we've changed spiritually as individuals & how this has had a measurable impact on spirited society itself. One social program we know contributes measurably to communal capitalistic life is sustained education in the liberal arts & sciences. We also know that our mobile phones can tell us how we are physically as this is increasingly seen to empower our personal fitness of mind within our grounded bodies. The ancient Latin expression remains true today, mens sana in corpore sano, or, a healthy mind in a healthy body. To extrapolate to the macro, this means a healthy individual in a healthy society, where mind & body are reflected in both the personal & governing states of spiritual well-being. Of course, we must all agree on the aspects of what this all means, & that is what makes democracies potent. Charity & philanthropy in this sense mean not only tangible contributions to others within society but also intangible love we demonstrate for one another through spiritual good deeds.

CONSCIOUS SELF-RULE & MINDFUL POLICING

While the limits of the rules-based system are clear, it is the best system we have in democracies & worldwide. It allows us for the most part to govern ourselves, depending on our will to participating, particularly in voting but also in philanthropy. The police, when implementing corrections to deviations from the law, notably with reference to narcotics infractions, are well educated in the liberal arts & sciences, as well as receiving training so that they are consciously mindful of human rights of the citizens within the state. Ideally, the police should also inherit the responsibilities of militaries & enforce border regulations, preferably unarmed, as the police in Britain generally do not carry weapons. This police behaviour is a sign of societal faith in pacific relations between friendly neighbours across & within borders. It is also a sign of faith in ourselves' latent spiritual potential for harmonious relations & G-d itself. Militaries, by virtue of the violently competitive nature of the international arena, are less inclined than police to respect human rights. Efficient police, born in democracies, are at the gateway to a better world as they assume military responsibilities. They have also contributed, as domestically-based *peace officers*, to the formation of international rules & regulations to prevent conflict & promote peacekeeping.

Thus people should respect police & the burden of laws of peace they carry for society & attempt to internalize these legal norms regulating our behaviour & preventing internal conflicts. This will lighten the burden of activity on the police & free them to be more mediators of conflicts than enforcers of laws. We should enforce laws in our own behaviour & live in peace intuitively with one another. This is a form & chance for mindful self policing (consciously cooperative with police), while recognizing the ego limits & spiritual potentialities our legal system could allow to blossom.

In the meantime of our spiritual growth, we are bogged down by the limits of prison/jail system, that hides away the ill of our society & has limited means to reform them, while emanating some negative energy into society from ill personalities. Efforts to introduce meditation into prisons as a method of reform have also been limited. More effects in meditation are being applied to conflict veterans dealing with PTSD, notably through a Transcendental Meditation™ approach. This nonetheless is encouraging for the prison system's rehabilitation strategies, & implies a manner of regular meditation in the normal domestic world that prevent the aberrations of behaviour that lead to violent crime, & to the necessity of the prison/jail system. Even so, the well & reformed prison inmate stands at the metaphorical gateway to the next world of democratic participation, one of being meditatively at harmony with themselves & others.

CONSCIOUS SPIRITUAL HEALTH & MINDFUL MEDITATION

Here we will deal with holistic solutions for conscious spiritual health & mindful meditation, to allow the individual citizen to dig deeper into their emotions & intellect so as to consciously reflect positively in their mindfully chosen society. Spiritual health is indeed a measure of finding where you are in yourself & your community & realizing your best attributes to contribute better to society at large. It is about respecting others & the laws of society & nature (sometimes hierarchical), while working to internalize those legal norms into our horizontal collective behaviour in a democratically consensual self-policing manner. The purpose of this is to generate domestic nation state utopias that resonate around & across the world.

But of course, as all politics is local, positive vibrations start at home with the individual self. These can be vibrantly amplified by the process of meditation. Meditation involves sitting quietly alone or with others, upright or cross-legged in a manner so that blood flow is upright, not laying down. There are other activities we need to do, such as sleep or sex, laying down, but meditation is a disciplined free flowing of circulation that is a sort of mental activity that lets go of mental activity, while conscious of the world around us, it relaxes the mind while remaining alert to the body's processes & general health. People non focus in different manners while meditating, a common favorite is the TM™ method from India where a mantra is assigned that one repeats. This is a peaceful, perhaps familiar word with a positive resonation that at once focuses & calms the body, releasing pent up tensions & allowing the brain to re-energize. Many people are familiar with the word OM, the Buddhist invocation of the natural current that runs through all being, but stops short of ascribing the name G-d to it, that remains elusive in all esoteric paths of the various spiritual religions.

One can also meditate generally on positive things, such as spiritual religious lessons, or on personal development issues or stumbling blocks in relationships, but these tend to intellectualize the spirit, to lower it to the mental realm of body rather than elevate the spirit above our intense minds into the collective, even communal consciousness. The secret to letting go is to release intensity to relax the mind so as to save it for intellectual or simple forgotten work later. Letting go does not necessarily sacrifice one's ego to the community superego, but in fact can generate more vigourous individual realizations without aggression but spiritual atonement with humans & nature itself. Enjoying a coffee could have some meditative effects but the ironic discipline of the non intensity of invoking a positive mantra is relatively proven to emanate the individual positively within their chosen society at the most & at the minimum within due legal bounds of said society.

There are many other meditative activities that stimulate different parts of the body, such as sexual, fitness, digesting a book or viewing TV or film. These depend on different contexts & can be done alone or together & must require consensus & respect. But it is absolute silence or repeated invocation of a single mantra that releases the mind from the stress of wound-up intellectual or insecure/repressed sexualities. Fitness is nonetheless a close relative of meditation since it remains focused without necessarily an intellectual concentration. It also serves as a median point between sexuality channeling & meditation, whose aspects are reflected also in one another in different manners conscious & unconscious. All these activities can heighten our unconscious potentials, leading to enlightenment of sorts, but it is meditation that most effectively focuses those energies in reserve into productive activity later, after meditation. These activities may be more practical than one expects, rather than experiencing divine revelations or epiphanies of the mystical measure, but it does not exclude these experiences either, & could emphasize them.

But TM leaves that to the individual choice rather than organizing into a religion of spiritualities, that could or could not resemble a cult as many esoteric sects are known as corrupt. In fact, in the realm of esoterics, egos can be as pronounced as in organized religions, leading to what we now witness as postmodern fragmentations of societal togetherness. It is better that, having once meditated, individuals find commonalities with one another & focus on those rather than their differences. This strengthens communities & societies at large while boding well for international relations & the health of the nature of the planet we have the privilege to live on. Meditation is about consciously, mindfully respecting it & ourselves.

DALENA LORENZO

POSTFACE

This short treatise is about recognizing the sanctity of your life, through meditation that permits you to find yourself, release your inner potential & bound energetically into your chosen individuality & society. It is about being globally conscious in the high-minded spirit of your personality while down to earth in by being a locally mindful citizen in your own respective society. It is about having at once let go of the fears & inhibitions that hold yourself down, & rather avoiding worrying too excessively about the constraints of society's relatively ancient, but not necessarily outdated structures. In fact, meditation can help you see , as the current OM runs through all things, that G-d's will is manifest in a relatively enlightened manner in various civilizations throughout successive centuries.

We continue to inherit these wisdom traditions & their sustainable reflection in lesser but continually important bureaucratic manifestations that maintain & institute the laws of the land, allowing them to thrive through our mindful consciousness to see things easily & celebrate life's simplicities, particularly in nature. This often occurs via meditation, while opening new vistas on the horizon of our domestic & international relationships, be they in family, patriotic community or reflective of a regional evolving sovereignty of a multiple state grouping or international organization that sets an original precedent for peace between many individual states (OSCE). Surely we all enjoy ample time in our ancient lives to reflect on how we can best give to society.

Patriotism, a subject of further exploration, in this sense is a measure of individual & societal self-definition, that is, finding oneself from within rather than from the often false mirror appearance of a seemingly antagonistic neighbour. Neighbourly relations are perhaps more complex than can be discoursed upon here in this short treatise.

GLOBALLY CONSCIOUS SPIRIT, LOCALLY MINDFUL CITIZEN

DALENA LORENZO

GLOBALLY CONSCIOUS SPIRIT, LOCALLY MINDFUL CITIZEN

DALENA LORENZO

www.ingramcontent.com/pod-product-compliance
Lightning Source LLC
Chambersburg PA
CBHW071202240526
45470CB00017B/1229